Beaux Arts New York

Augustus Saint-Gauden's William Tecumseh Sherman monument at the north end of Manhattan's Grand Army Plaza is an incomparable example of Beaux Arts style. The gilded bronze group was mounted on its granite base designed by Charles F. McKim in 1903. A plaster version of the Sherman monument, replete with the palm-bearing figure of Victory, is shown here on display in the Grand Palais during the Exposition Universelle held in Paris in 1900. ROGER-VIOLLET

Beaux Arts New York

DAVID GARRARD LOWE

WHITNEY LIBRARY OF DESIGN

An Imprint of Watson-Guptill Publications | *New York*

First published in 1998 by Whitney Library of Design,
an imprint of Watson-Guptill Publications, a division of BPI Communications, Inc.,
1515 Broadway, New York, NY 10036

ISBN 0-8230-0481-3

Library of Congress Cataloging-in-Publication Data
Lowe, David Garrard.
        Beaux arts New York / David Garrard Lowe.
            p.   cm.
        Based on an exhibition held at the PaineWebber Art Gallery.
        Includes bibliographical references.
        ISBN 0-8230-0481-3 (paper)
1. Eclecticism in architecture—New York (State)—New York.
2. Architecture, Modern—19th century—New York (State)—New York.
3. Architecture, Modern—20th century—New York (State)—New York.
4. New York (N.Y.)—Buildings, structures, etc.   I. PaineWebber Art Gallery. II. Title.
NA735.N5L69 1998   98-3935
720'.9747'10904—dc21   CIP

Manufactured in the United States of America

First printing, 1998

1 2 3 4 5 6 7 8 9 / 06 05 04 03 02 01 00 99 98

Editor: *Micaela Porta*
Designer: *Derek Bacchus*
Production Manager: *Ellen Greene*

Acknowledgments

Sally Forbes has been a part of this book since its birth as an exhibition at the Paine Webber Art Gallery in New York. Every step of the way, her knowledge of pictures and where to find them, her wise judgment of words and illustrations, and her sense of this city, have been irreplaceable elements of this project.

I would like also to thank Colin Thomson, director of the Paine Webber Art Gallery, where the exhibition "Beaux Arts New York" was mounted, and Suzanne Gyorgy, his predecessor.

Tracking down the illustrations for this book proved to be a wonderful treasure hunt. Along the way many people helped. In particular I would like to thank Janet Parks, Curator of Drawings at the Avery Architectural and Fine Arts Library of Columbia University; Wendy Shadwell, Curator of Prints at the New-York Historical Society; Marguerite Lavin, licensing specialist of the Museum of the City of New York; Robert Sink of the New York Public Library; Gordon McCollum of the American Architectural Archives; John Frazier of the Pierpont Morgan Library; Katherine M. Gerlaugh of The Frick Collection; Joseph Jackson, librarian of the New York Yacht Club; the Very Reverend Harry H. Pritchett, Jr., Dean of the Cathedral of St. John the Divine; John Zukowsky and Luigi Mumford of the Art Institute of Chicago; Sherry Birk of the Octagon Museum; Charles Young of the Queens Library; Ford Peatross, Curator of Architecture, Library of Congress; Sam Daniel, reference specialist, Prints and Photographs Division, Library of Congress; Hennie Imberman of Congregation Shearith Israel; Mark Altherr, President of the Down Town Association; Deborah Bershad of the Art Commission; Robert Tuggle and John Pennino of the Metropolitan Opera Archives; William D. Moore of the Livingston Masonic Library; Manny Strumpf of the National Park Service; Father Paul Robichaud, C.P.S., Archivist of the Paulist Fathers; Mark Piel of the New York Society Library; Annette Fern and Michael T. Dumas of the Harvard Theatre Library; Mrs. Barea Lamb Seeley; Richard Jay Hutto; and Chris Kilduff of Speed Graphics, Inc.

Numerous friends and colleagues have given of their knowledge and time in the making of this book. I would like to name Richard E. Slavin III, archivist of F. Schumacher & Co.; the Reverend Peter Laarman, pastor of Judson Memorial Church; Susan Tunick of the Friends of Terra Cotta; Paul Hayden, curator of the Seventh Regiment Armory; Jean Wiart of LMC Corp.; O. Alden James, President of the National Arts Club; Curt Gathje of The Plaza Hotel; Victor Alonzo of Objets Plus, Inc.; Michael Patrick of Harvey & Co. Antiques; Adrienne Bresnan; Jean Bubley; Timothy Beard; James H. Burke; John Cadenhead; James F. McCollom; and James W. Guedry.

A very special word of thanks must go to Noah Lukeman, who, after viewing the exhibition "Beaux Arts New York," had the imagination to see it as a book. Finally, I would like to thank the Reverend Allan Bevier Warren, III, rector of the Church of the Resurrection, whose parish house shelters the Beaux Arts Alliance, an organization that cherishes the wondrous world shown on these pages.

Contents

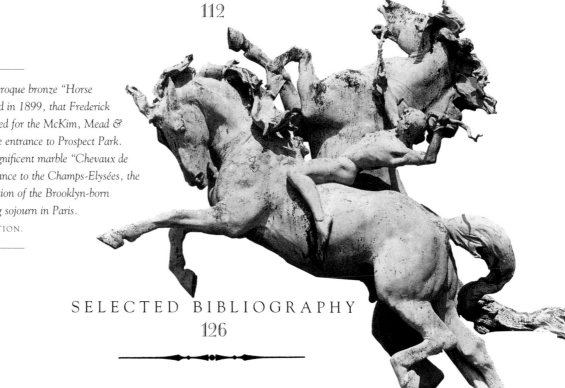

One of a pair of baroque bronze "Horse Tamers," completed in 1899, that Frederick MacMonnies created for the McKim, Mead & White's Park Circle entrance to Prospect Park. Inspired by the magnificent marble "Chevaux de Marly" at the entrance to the Champs-Elysées, the statues are a reflection of the Brooklyn-born MacMonnies's long sojourn in Paris.

PRIVATE COLLECTION.

Introduction

"IN PARIS," THAT PERSPICACIOUS New Yorker, Edith Wharton, wrote in the first chapter of her seminal book on design, *The Decoration of Houses*, "it is impossible to take even a short walk without finding inspiration in those admirable buildings, public and private, religious and secular, that bear the stamp of the most refined taste the world has known since the decline of the arts in Italy." Paris and France are rarely absent from the continuing drama that is the history of New York City. The Huguenots were here from the very beginning with Peter Minuit, who became governor of New Amsterdam in 1626. These French Protestants were to give the city deForests and Jays, Lorillards and Goelets. And there would also be great Roman Catholic families—the La Farges, Couderts, and Bouviers—swept to Manhattan by the storms swirling around the French Revolution and Napoleon Bonaparte. Almost always, the French brought to the city a touch of elegance, whether they were silversmiths like the Le Roux family or emigré cabinetmakers like Charles-Honoré Lannuier who, when he arrived in New York in 1803, immediately advertised that he made furniture "in the newest and latest French fashion." The first theater in New York, the Park, was designed by two Frenchmen, and the advent of serious dining in the city can be dated from the opening on William Street in 1827 of the first Delmonico's. Though the family was of Swiss-Italian background, their French menu transported eager New Yorkers from the world of roast turkey to that of "dinde à la Lyonnaise."

New Yorkers seem to have always gone to Paris and to have fallen in love with it. At

The Arc de Triomphe du Carrousel, Paris, begun in 1806, was designed by Fontaine and Percier to commemorate the victories of Napoleon I.
ROGER-VIOLLET.

the birth of the Republic, Gouverneur Morris was appointed in 1792 by George Washington to succeed Thomas Jefferson as American Minister in Paris. Morris, a patrician who spoke perfect French, became a collector of French furniture and decorative objects, which ultimately filled his house, "Morrisana," in the Bronx. The first American to become a serious art student in Paris, John Vanderlyn, was sent there at the end of the 18th century by no less a personage than Aaron Burr. Upon his return to New York in 1815, Vanderlyn constructed the city's first public art gallery, a rotunda in which to display his enormous panorama of the château and gardens of Versailles. By the time of the Civil War, New York ladies—Lion Gardiners, Schermerhorns, and Iselins—were annually visiting Worth on the rue de la Paix for gowns of gauze, velvet, and tulle to be worn at dinners and balls during the coming season.

The physical reality of the French presence in New York embraces some of the city's most cherished sites. These range from the carved wooden reredos designed by Pierre L'Enfant behind the altar of St. Paul's Chapel on lower Broadway to City Hall, whose sophisticated continental style reveals the familiarity of its co-architect, Joseph-Francois Mangin, with the private houses of Paris, to the old emporiums of Arnold Constable and Lord & Taylor along the Ladies' Mile on Broadway between 14th and 23rd streets, where the high mansard roofs of the

1860s reflect New Yorkers' fascination with the Second Empire opulence of Napoleon III and his Empress, Eugénie. And always, inescapably, there is the 151-foot-high statue in the harbor sculpted by Frédéric-Auguste Bartholdi into an unsurpassed personification of Liberty. Presented by the people of France to the United States to commemorate the centennial of

View of the Palais du Louvre's Cour Napoleon showing the north wing constructed by Napoleon III in the 19th century from designs by Visconti and Lefuel. ROGER-VIOLLET.

the Declaration of Independence, the figure also celebrates the bonds between the two nations.

Thus, when in 1883 the new house that Richard Morris Hunt designed for the William K. Vanderbilts at the northwest corner of Fifth Avenue and 52nd Street introduced the full panoply of Beaux Arts architecture into New York, the ground had been well prepared for it. A four-story French Renaissance château echoing Chenonceau and Blois, the pale limestone edifice was like a blazing lantern set down amid the somber brownstone of old New York. With its graceful ogee moldings, slender turret embellished with fleurs-de-lis, and high blue-slate roof, the Vanderbilt mansion signified a sea change in Gotham's taste. The Beaux Arts style would dominate the architecture of New York until the epoch it exemplified died in the trenches of the First World War, in the mud of Ypres and upon the barbed wire of Verdun.

Significantly, both the château's chatelaine, Alva Erskine Smith Vanderbilt, and its architect had spent their formative years in Paris. Alva's father, a wealthy Mobile, Alabama, cotton merchant, had taken his family to the French capital after having been ruined by the Civil War. Hunt's sojourn in Paris had been the result of his rich, recently widowed mother's desire to trade the drab Puritanism of New England for the sparkling charms of Paris. When, in 1845, he was admitted to the École des Beaux-Arts on the Left Bank of the Seine, Hunt became a cultural pioneer. He was the first American to enter the architectural section of the famed school that had been formed in 1819 from the Académie Royale de Peinture et Sculpture and the Académie Royale d'Architecture. "Aujourd'hui nous commençons bien étudier l'architecture" (today we begin truly to study architecture), he had inscribed in his diary as he prepared for his entrance exams. The "we" may be said to have stood for three generations of American architects who would follow him through the school's gates on the rue Bonaparte. To understand the full significance of Hunt's matriculation at the École, one has only to remember that the second American architect to enter was Henry Hobson Richardson, from whose hand came such Romanesque Revival monuments as Boston's Trinity Church, and that the third was Charles F. McKim, creator of that marvel of the age of steam, Pennsylvania Station.

The genius of the École des Beaux-Arts derived from its creative mix of the academic and professional worlds. At the École itself students attended lectures on architectural theory, as well as courses in engineering, materials, and urban planning. It was also at the École that the all-important sketches had to be completed within twelve hours and the finished drawings that were to be handed in within two months were assigned. At the core of its instruction was the dictum that the ultimate expression of beauty in architecture was the classical. (In the 1860s the hegemony of classicism had briefly been challenged by advocates of the Gothic, and that style was never totally dismissed by the École.) Classicism remained the supreme ideal, and by classicism the professors of the École meant not only the buildings of ancient Greece and Rome, but also the architecture of the Italian and French Renaissance. In a typically French appeal to reason, the École proclaimed that it could be demonstrated by logic that the proportion and forms of the classical, such as the five orders—Tuscan, Doric, Ionic, Corinthian, and Composite—were the eternal norms of architectural design. They were as real as the laws of physics, according to the École. The liberating result of this belief was that the École never advocated copying the structures of the past. There was no need for this, for classicism was alive and well and living in Paris. It had formed the Parthenon in Athens and St. Peter's in Rome, and just as assuredly it was an appropriate style for skyscrapers and powerhouses.

But the paramount glory of the École was the ateliers headed by established architects. Here twenty or so students cooperately paid the atelier's rent, bought the fuel for its fireplaces and stoves, purchased the candles and kerosene to light it, and paid the patron who visited once or twice a week to judge and to give advice. Scattered across the neighborhood surrounding the École in such streets as the rue de Seine, the rue Jacob, and the rue du Four, the joie de vivre and camaraderie of the ateliers was fondly remembered by the Americans who passed through them. Their spirit would be recreated in the offices of some of New York's greatest architectural firms, including that of Hunt; McKim, Mead & White; and Carrère & Hastings.

If in aesthetic theory the École looked back to the classical for inspiration, on its prac-

The grand staircase of Charles Garnier's Paris Opera, built between 1861 and 1875. ROGER-VIOLLET.

tical side it boldly embraced the future, accepting every new material and technique of construction: iron, steel, plate glass, rivets, the elevator. There was no sense of the fusty or the retrograde about Laloux's Gare d'Orsay or Garnier's Opera. Indeed, it is this taut combination of state-of-the-art construction clothed in forms perfected by the architects of the temples upon the Acropolis in Athens and of the palaces of Rome that give Beaux Arts buildings their structural vitality and their aesthetic magnetism. It is this very combination that sparks the frisson felt by the commuter beneath the electric stars in Grand Central Terminal's colossal concourse, and that makes the aerial terra cotta–clad Woolworth Building a thing of perennial beauty.

The Beaux Arts style came to America and to New York at precisely the right moment. It was the era when the external immigration from Europe and the internal movement from America's farms and small towns transformed the United States from a rural into an urban nation. Nowhere was this change more startlingly evident than in New York. Situated on islands where the rail lines—the New York Central and the Pennsylvania—of the vast North American land mass met the sea upon which the steam ships of the fabled fleets of Cunard and

13

the French Line carried passengers to Liverpool and Cherbourg, New York by the 1880s was the de facto capital of the United States. This ascendancy was abetted by those inventions that are the apex of the Industrial Revolution: the telephone, the electric light, and the elevator. All had made their appearance in the city by the early 1880s. Combined, they permitted compa-

The Gare d'Orsay, designed by Victor Laloux, opened in 1900. It is now the Musée d'Orsay. ROGER-VIOLLET.

nies to consolidate their offices in one place and construct edifices tall enough to hold the enormous number of workers thus gathered together. The advent in the 1870s of the steam-driven Third and Sixth Avenue El lines made it convenient for the workers scattered across the face of the metropolis to reach these towering hives. The office buildings of the Beaux Arts era—the Singer, the Flatiron, the Metropolitan Life—were testimonials to this achievement. No wonder on a visit to New York in 1913, the English poet, Rupert Brooke, wrote, "I have often noticed that in the early morning, and again for a little about sunset, the sky-scrapers are no longer merely the means and local convenience for men to pursue their purposes, but acquire that characteristic of the great buildings of the world, an existence and meaning of their own."

14 New York's population, 123,000 in 1820, had grown to 1,080,330 by 1860. Then in

1890 it surpassed 2 million and, with the consolidation that came with the annexation of Brooklyn, Queens, Staten Island, and the Bronx in 1898, it reached an astounding 3.1 million. Its old rivals for national supremacy—Boston and Philadelphia—were left in the dust, and its young rival, Chicago, became the Second City. Finance, commerce, and the arts were all centered in the metropolis of the Empire State. The writer Hamlin Garland on a trip from Chicago, where he was living, to New York saw clearly the new American landscape:

> *On my return to New York City in January, 1900, I found it in the midst of rebuilding, and I soon discovered that changes in the literary and artistic world were keeping pace with the swift transformations of the business world. New publishing houses were being established and new magazines. . . . The aesthetic life of all America was centralizing, with appalling rapidity, on this small island. The inland writer, like the inland publisher, was persuaded that in order to gain a national reputation he must speak from Manhattan.*

It is therefore not surprising that when Charles F. McKim announced to his parents that he was leaving Philadelphia for New York, his father approved. "One is a great provincial town," the elder McKim observed, "the other is a metropolitan city."

Provincial was not a word in the vocabulary of the École des Beaux-Arts. Its home was Paris, a city that celebrates urbanity. The experience of living in the French capital would have a profound effect on every American architect who studied there. This was the city of Baron Haussmann's magnificent boulevards; of the 900-room Grand Hotel that set the standard for the world's new caravansaries; of Maxim's; of the Arc de Triomphe; of the Eiffel Tower; of the Luxembourg Gardens; and of the sumptuous new private palaces rising on the Champs-Elysées and the Avenue des Bois. The presence of the City of Light is palpable in the work of Americans who studied there like Whitney Warren, Ernest Flagg, and John Carrère, and also of those Beaux Arts architects, like Stanford White, who did not attend the school, but grew to love the city. Their dream was to transfer to New York on the Hudson the shimmering world of Paris on the Seine.

And Paris provided something else. For Americans it was the gateway to

Gustave Eiffel's 984-foot-tall tower was the centerpiece of the great exhibition held in Paris in 1889 to celebrate the centennial of the French Revolution. ROGER-VIOLLET.

Rome. The ultimate prize at the École was the Prix de Rome, which allowed students to study for three years at the French Academy in the Villa Medici. It is of profound significance that Hunt and McKim strove to establish an American Academy in the Eternal City. Added to the wonders of Paris, the art and opulence of Rome—of the Sistine Chapel, the Piazza Navona, and the Palazzo Farnese—taught Americans that less was not more, but that indeed more was more. It was an essential lesson for citizens of a nation infatuated with the spare and the simple. After seeing LeBrun's "Galerie des Glaces" at Versailles and Bernini's baldachino at St. Peter's, architects could return to New York prepared to build on a scale and with the complexity required by the burgeoning city. This had been beyond the reach of the crafters of Egyptian Revival prisons,

Gothic Revival cottages, and Tuscan villas, the styles that had held sway before Beaux Arts.

Furthermore, because of their experience of Paris and Rome—of Latin civilization— the Beaux Arts architects reveled in rich materials, in red- and purple- and green-veined marbles, in gilded capitals, in the pale palette of limestone, and in shaped bronze. They employed frescoes and pleasing images of the botanical world—garlands of roses, sheaves of wheat, the acanthus leaf—and of the animal world—rams, eagles, lions' heads. Above all, they embraced that standard of perfection, the human form itself. Their buildings are embellished with caryatids and Greek and Roman gods and goddesses, with putti and angels.

It was this new Beaux Arts city that, on his last visit to his hometown in the spring of 1905, both dazzled and abashed Henry James. He recorded his myriad sensations in *The American Scene:*

> *"There is the beauty of light and air, the great scale of space, and, seen far away to the west, the open gates of the Hudson, majestic in their degree, even at a distance, and announcing still nobler things. But the real appeal, unmistakably, is in the note of vehemence in the local life . . . for it is in the appeal of a particular type of dauntless power. The aspect the power wears then is indescribable; it is the power of the most extravagant of cities, rejoicing, as with the voice of the morning, in its unsurpassable conditions. . . .*

It was the Beaux Arts that found New York a city of sooty brownstone and left it one of bright marble, furnished it with palaces and galleries, caravansaries and public monuments. It was the Beaux Arts style that made New York dare to be extravagant and also to be beautiful.

Chapter One

Grand Entrances

THE APPROACH TO NEW YORK in the age of the Beaux Arts combined marvelous ceremony and high drama. There was the first distant view, the steady approach as Gotham grew larger and larger, and then the arrival in the very heart of the place itself. If one came by sea, there was that spine-tingling sighting of the Statue of Liberty, then glimpses of lower Manhattan's towers, structures like nothing else on the earth, and the stately glide up the Hudson to a pier that was part of the buzzing hive of city life. The name of the ships of that era—the *Mauretania, Kronprinzessen Cecilie, La Savoie*—reverberate like labels from great vineyards. The railroads, too, were freighted with romance, and their sumptuous trains—the Sunset Limited, Royal Blue, Twentieth Century Limited—made up of palace cars and Pullman dining cars and observation cars arrived at stations as spectacular as anything dreamt of in the Rome of the Caesars or at Versailles. Stepping into Pennsylvania Station or Grand Central Terminal, the traveler knew that this was not a hamlet in Kansas, but a metropolis of unquestionable consequence.

Pennsylvania Station's travertine-sheathed general waiting room was inspired by the tepidarium—the chamber between the hot and cold rooms—of Rome's Baths of Caracalla and was as large as the nave of St. Peter's Basilica. Below the waiting room's thermal windows were maps of the Pennsylvania's rail network by the artist Jules Guerin. AVERY ARCHITECTURE AND FINE ARTS LIBRARY.

Not only was
Pennsylvania Station
Beaux Arts in style,
but so were many of
the trains that served
it. A dazzling example
of a palace on wheels
was the Louis XV–
style private car that
the Pullman Company
fashioned in 1897
for Mexican leader
Porfirio Diaz.
PRIVATE COLLECTION.

When Pennsylvania Station opened in the autumn of 1910, the architect, Charles F. McKim, could not witness the awestruck crowds that gathered to admire his masterpiece. (McKim had died two years before.) No New York structure since the Brooklyn Bridge had made such an impact. The 35-foot-high Roman Doric colonnade stretching along Seventh Avenue from 32nd to 33rd streets was, like the bridge itself, proclaimed a gate to the metropolis. The station's pink granite walls enclosed eight acres.

The station's train concourse —340 feet long and 210 feet wide—was a Beaux Arts triumph, daringly echoing the waiting room's masonry and plaster forms in iron and glass. It was the technological and design climax of the 19th century's love affair with glass and metal construction, which had begun with the Crystal Palace Joseph Paxton designed for London's Great Exhibition of 1851. This seminal room was lost with the demolition of Pennsylvania Station that began in 1963.

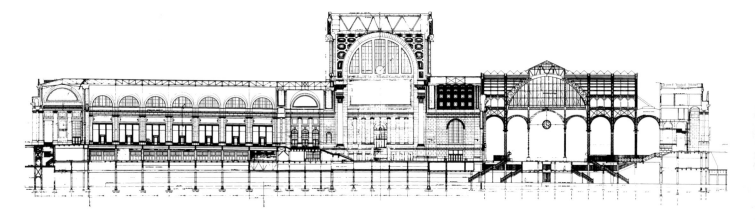

ABOVE: *Blueprint of a view of Pennsylvania Station. Construction on the station began in 1906, though the all-important tunnels under the Hudson that linked it to the railroad's New Jersey tracks were begun two years earlier.*

The station unabashedly proclaimed that the Pennsylvania had entered Manhattan, once the exclusive baili-wick of the Vanderbilts' New York Central. AVERY ARCHITECTURE AND FINE ARTS LIBRARY.

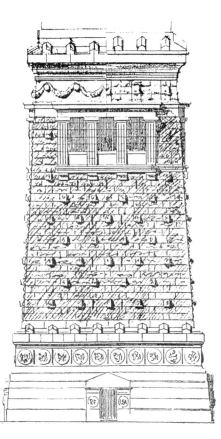

LEFT AND BELOW: *With Ellis Island, the towers of Lower Manhattan, and the Statue of Liberty, the Beaux Arts style transformed the face of New York's harbor. By the beginning of the 1880s, Richard Morris Hunt— the first American to attend the architecture section of the École des Beaux-Arts—had been selected to design the base of Frédéric-Auguste Bartholdi's Statue of Liberty. Among Hunt's numerous sketches for the project is this one of 1883, which features intricate rustication and a pattern of projecting stone blocks.* PRIVATE COLLECTIONS.

23

ABOVE: *The Cunard Line's 31,000-ton* Lusitania *— launched in 1907 — outbound on the Hudson River in 1909. The* Lusitania *and her sister ship, the* Mauretania, *had opulent Edwardian Louis XVI–style interiors designed to appeal to rich Americans who lived in Beaux Arts palaces. The* Lusitania *was sunk by a German U-boat off the Irish coast on May 7, 1915.*
PRIVATE COLLECTION.

RIGHT: *The interiors of Cunard's* Aquitania *— launched in 1914 — were the work of the Frenchman Charles Mewes and his École des Beaux-Arts–trained English partner, Arthur Davis. For the ship's public spaces, such as the First Class Stairway, Mewes employed a restrained French-inspired grandeur of the kind he had created for the Ritz hotels in Paris and London.*
PRIVATE COLLECTION.

ABOVE: *The main building of the United States Immigration Station on Ellis Island presents a monumental triple-triumphal arch entryway to those coming to a new land. In the best Beaux Arts tradition, the edifice is adorned with appropriate ornament; in this case, American eagles. The 1898 brick-and-limestone structure was one of five buildings on the island designed by Boring & Tilton. William A. Boring, the senior partner, was head of Columbia's School of Architecture. The steamboats in this 1905 photograph carried newly arrived immigrants from the Hudson River piers, where they had disembarked after their trans-Atlantic crossing, to Ellis Island. Once the immigrants had passed the required medical and other tests and had been cleared to enter the United States, the boats ferried them to Manhattan.* PRIVATE COLLECTION.

LEFT: *The registry room in the main building has a 62-foot-high ceiling of Guastavino tile. The structure, restored in 1991, is now part of the Ellis Island National Monument.* NATIONAL PARK SERVICE.

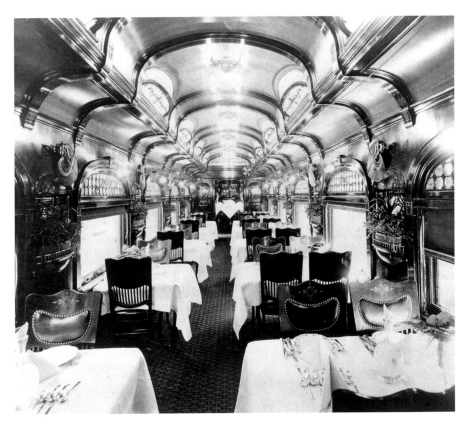

ABOVE: *Dining car on the New York Central's first Twentieth Century Limited, inaugurated in 1902. The car, designed in 1896, was built by the Pullman Company. The Twentieth Century made a crack 18-hour run between Grand Central and Chicago's LaSalle Street Station daily.* PRIVATE COLLECTION.

OPPOSITE: *Grand Central Terminal on 42nd Street at Park Avenue was built between 1902 and 1913 by Reed & Stem and Warren & Wetmore. Its magnificent Indiana limestone façade of paired columns and triple arches was designed as a triumphal gate to New York City. It is topped by Jules* Coutan's *48-foot-high sculptural group, with, approximately at its center, Mercury, the Roman god of commerce.* PHOTOGRAPH BY MELANIE FORBES.

The original sketch for the facade of the Grand Central Terminal by Whitney Warren 1910

ABOVE, RIGHT: *The main concourse of Grand Central Terminal—an awesome 125 feet wide and 385 feet long—has walls of artificial Caen stone, decorative elements in Bottocino marble, and a floor of Tennessee marble. The power of this great room derives from Whitney Warren's brilliant Beaux Arts stratagem of creating the sense of a column-enclosed classical hall, when, in fact, its piers have a startling, almost Art Deco spareness about them. They soar, without capitals, 125 feet to a restrained entablature from which springs a vaulted ceiling decorated with electrically lit constellations of the zodiac conceived by the French painter, Paul Helleu.*
PRIVATE COLLECTION.

OPPOSITE: *In this 1919 view looking west on 42nd Street, Grand Central Terminal is on the right, while the tall mansard-roofed building in the background at Madison Avenue is the Hotel Manhattan of 1897, designed by Henry J. Hardenbergh. In front of Grand Central is the roof of the El station that served a spur of the Third Avenue line.*
LIBRARY OF CONGRESS.

© BY AMERICAN STUDIO N.Y. 1919
42 St LOOKING WEST FROM GRAND CENTRAL

29

This 1920 view north on Park Avenue shows the malls created just before the First World War, when the replacement of steam locomotives by electric ones made it practical to cover over the New York Central Railroad's open cut. The malls, which eloquently expressed the Beaux Arts ideals of the City Beautiful, were destroyed in 1927 when they were reduced to mere traffic islands by the widening of the streets on either side. On the right beyond St. Bartholomew's Church (Bertram Grosvenor Goodhue, 1919) is the 500-room Hotel Ambassador by Warren & Wetmore. The chic hostelry opened in 1921 and was demolished in the 1960s.

————◆——◆——◆————

Chapter Two

Magnificent Caravansaries

THE RAILWAY STATION AND THE HOTEL were the two most important new building types developed in the 19th century. New York had boasted large hotels as early as 1836, when Isaiah Rogers designed the granite 300-room Astor House on Broadway near City Hall. The Astor House caused a stir with its up-to-date indoor plumbing. In time it was joined by the six-story Fifth Avenue Hotel facing Madison Square, the first hotel to have an elevator, and by the Second Empire–style Park Avenue Hotel on 33rd Street. But it was left for the Beaux Arts to create a truly sensational palace hotel with Henry J. Hardenbergh's 530-room Waldorf at Fifth Avenue and 33rd Street, which opened in 1893. It was joined four years later by the even larger Astoria to complete the creation of what old New Yorkers always called "The Hyphen." With its Palm Garden, its Rose and Empire rooms, its Men's Cafe, and, above all, its 300-foot-long marble-sheathed Peacock Alley, the Waldorf-Astoria set a new standard of scale and opulence. The Astor family would build a number of splendid caravansaries in New York, including the handsome Knickerbocker at Broadway and 42nd Street. There was something curiously democratic about these grand hotels. E. I. Zeisloft, in his 1899

Henry J. Hardenbergh's colossal 1,000-room Waldorf-Astoria Hotel, which occupied the block on Fifth Avenue between 33rd and 34th streets, was actually two hotels, the Waldorf, completed in 1893, and the Astoria, which opened in 1897. In this 1898 view looking south, the A. T. Stewart mansion rises just across 34th Street from the hotel while the impressive brick building with awnings is the exclusive New York Club. The Waldorf-Astoria was demolished in 1929 to make way for the Empire State Building.
LIBRARY OF CONGRESS.

book, *The New Metropolis*, noted that even in a spot as posh as Peacock Alley any man, "provided he is well dressed, may sit about these corridors night after night." But even the glitter of the Waldorf-Astoria was outshone on October 1, 1907, when Hardenbergh's new Plaza Hotel opened. When the throng, which included Mr. and Mrs. Alfred Gwynne Vanderbilt, Oliver Harriman, and Mr. and Mrs. George Jay Gould, entered Hardenbergh's French Renaissance masterpiece, they moved among Louis XVI furniture, walked upon Savonnerie carpets, while overhead Baccarat crystal chandeliers lit their way. So that there would be no jarring note, the Plaza's footmen were attired in gold and fawn livery with gold lace at throat and wrists, while the doorman was in full French court attire replete with black satin breeches and long black silk stockings. Lined up on the Fifth Avenue side of the hotel were high green-and-red cabs imported from France, New York's first metered gasoline-driven taxis.

While the development of the New York hotel followed a comparatively smooth course, such was not the case with the apartment building. Though as early as 1857, the architect Calvert Vaux had proposed that prosperous New Yorkers should give up their individual dwellings and live "à la française"—that is, in apartments—the American resistance to the so-called "French flat" was fierce. When Vaux made his proposal, such physical arrangements could be found only in the tenements that housed the poor. The idea seemed both foreign and immoral. But, in time, the development of the elevator, which made living on high floors with views practical, and the conveniences of the services offered by apartment houses banished such prejudices. By the first decade of this century, princely Beaux Arts apartment buildings, such as the Alwyn Court, offered 34-room suites as luxurious as almost any New York mansion.

LEFT: *The Plaza Hotel, Central Park South near Fifth Avenue, another Hardenbergh masterpiece, opened in 1907.* PRIVATE COLLECTION.

BELOW, LEFT AND RIGHT: *The original decor given to a number of the Plaza's public rooms by the French firm of L. Alavoine et Cie. is still intact in these 1913 photographs.* PRIVATE COLLECTION.

35

OPPOSITE: *Located at the southwest corner of Fifth Avenue and 44th Street, the 11-story hotel that Stanford White designed for Louis Sherry was the result of the famed caterer's desire to have an establishment with a restaurant and full-service apartments. When it opened in* 1890, *its white-and-gold Louis XVI–style ballroom was hailed as the most beautiful in America. Sherry's served its last meal shortly after the First World War when, in the words of its proprietor, it succumbed to "Prohibition and Bolshevism."*

ABOVE: *The Astor Hotel, designed by Clinton & Russell and completed in 1904, occupied the block on Broadway between 44th and 45th streets. It brought Beaux Arts charm and dignity to Times Square. Both were lost when the hotel was demolished in the 1960s.*

In 1906, the Astor estate commissioned Maxfield Parrish to paint his "Old King Cole" for the new Knickerbocker Hotel, at the southeast corner of Broadway and 42nd Street. Among the hotel's occupants was the actor, composer, and playwright George M. Cohan. The Knickerbocker, designed by Marvin & Vavis, is now an office building, and King Cole reigns over the St. Regis. PRIVATE COLLECTION.

The fabled Italian tenor, Enrico Caruso, made his American debut at the Metropolitan Opera in Rigoletto in 1904. From then until his death at the age of 48 in 1921, he was the very personification of opera in New York. Caruso endowed any place he chose to live—the Knickerbocker and Ansonia hotels were two of his favorite domiciles—with luminescent glamour. He is shown here—standing second from left—with American friends in about 1910. PRIVATE COLLECTION.

OPPOSITE: If one were to select a single structure to illustrate the exuberant splendor that the Beaux Arts style brought to Gotham, that building would have to be the Ansonia Hotel at the northwest corner of Broadway and 73rd Street. William Earl Dodge Stokes employed a French architect, Paul E. M. DuBoy, to compose the seventeen stories of finely worked stone, balconies, rounded towers, and mansard roofs climaxing in elaborate chéneaux. When it opened in 1905, the hotel—which derived its name from Stokes's Ansonia Brass & Copper Company—immediately attracted residents of the caliber of Arturo Toscanini and Feodor Chaliapin. Though it has lost many of the Beaux Arts elements evident in this 1906 photograph, the Ansonia is still a delicious display of Parisian architectural joie de vivre. PRIVATE COLLECTION.

In 1906, the Astor estate commissioned Clinton & Russell, the architects of the Astor Hotel, to design the Florentine-inspired Apthorp Apartments. Filling the entire block on Broadway between 78th and 79th streets, the Apthorp boasts one of New York's most handsome interior courtyards.
PRIVATE COLLECTION.

OPPOSITE: *The Alwyn Court Apartments, at the southeast corner of Seventh Avenue and 58th Street, had been occupied for six years when this 1915 photograph was made. Harde & Short's exterior is a terra-cotta confection of French Renaissance details. The crowned salamanders above the doorway are the symbols of Francois I, one of the French monarchs who introduced Italian Renaissance architecture to France.*
PRIVATE COLLECTION.

ABOVE, LEFT: *The Commodore Hotel—like the Biltmore and Vanderbilt— reflected in its name its owner-ship by the New York Central. It was indeed a 1918 addition by Warren & Wetmore to the complex of buildings surrounding Grand Central called "Terminal City." The Commodore is now the Grand Hyatt.*
PRIVATE COLLECTION.

ABOVE, RIGHT: *Among the truly legendary New York hotels was the Ritz-Carlton, designed by Warren & Wetmore in 1910. Standing on Madison Avenue between 46th and 47th streets, its Robert Adam–inspired dining room, shown here, was one of the city's most fashionable gather-ing places. The Ritz-Carlton was razed in 1951 and replaced by an office building.*
PRIVATE COLLECTION.

OPPOSITE: *The emphatic massing and daringly high mansard roof—which echoed that of the older Plaza across Fifth Avenue—of McKim, Mead & White's Savoy Plaza proclaimed the continuing vitality of Beaux Arts design in the 1920s. This wonderfully urbane structure was destroyed in 1967 and replaced by the General Motors Building.*
PRIVATE COLLECTION.

42

43

The white marble edifice on Madison Square that houses the Appellate Division of the New York State Supreme Court might well be a Palladian villa wafted to Gotham from the Veneto. Constructed between 1896 and 1900, it exemplifies the Beaux Arts ideal of all of the arts working together to instruct and delight. Its architect, James Brown Lord, has embellished the Court's exterior with, appropriately, statues of great lawgivers—Moses, Solon, Confucius, among others—by notable sculptors, including Daniel Chester French and Philip Martiny. Its interior, by Herter Brothers, is enriched with murals and stunning stained glass. ART COMMISSION.

Chapter Three

Civic Pride

IN HIS MEMOIRS, *A King's Story*, the Duke of Windsor, recounting his awe at his tumultuous 1919 tickertape parade, recalls his surprise at discovering another aspect of New York: "Then suddenly the noise diminished; and the motor emerged from Broadway into a small park, in the center of which stood a low, two-story building of beautiful proportions. This, Mr. Wanamaker announced, was City Hall." New York's City Hall is not Beaux Arts, but an elegant Federal style survival from the beginning of the 19th century that reflects the small scale of the city at that time. So too Brooklyn's splendid Greek Revival Borough Hall of the middle of the 19th century represents perfectly that borough when it was a city of leafy streets and graceful neighborhoods of the type still to be found in Brooklyn Heights and Cobble Hill.

But with these exceptions, almost all of New York's memorable civic buildings are Beaux Arts. They mirror a metropolis whose population, once counted in the thousands, was now counted in the millions, a port whose customs duties in the era before the income tax of 1913 underwrote the operations of the federal government. These Beaux Arts edifices—McKim, Mead & White's soaring Municipal Building and Guy Lowell's Corinthian-columned New York County Courthouse, to name but two—are a civic continuum of the mansions and museums of Fifth Avenue, grand, proud, and architecturally boastful.

And there is another factor at play here. New Yorkers were stung by the all too frequent references to the palpable impermanence of America's cities. Edith Wharton, in her novel, *The Custom of the Country*, encapsulated this in the comments of the French Marquis de Chelles to his American wife: "You come . . . from towns as flimsy as paper, where the streets haven't had time to be named, and the buildings are demolished before they're dry." There is emphatically nothing flimsy about Cass Gilbert's statue-bedecked Custom House on Bowling Green or James Brown Lord's crystalline marble Appellate Court on Madison Square or Hoppin & Koen's Renaissance-domed old Police Headquarters on Centre Street. All deftly employ Beaux Arts stratagems of peerless materials, daz- zling craftsmanship, and ageless classical details to express permanence and civic continuity. They strive to make New York upon the Hudson, like Rome upon the Tiber, an eternal city.

PRIVATE COLLECTION

OPPOSITE AND LEFT: *One result of the 1898 consolidation of Brooklyn, Queens, Staten Island, the Bronx, and Manhattan into the City of New York was an enormous increase in city workers in Lower Manhattan. This sudden demand for office space resulted in the soaring 25-story Municipal Building that bridges Chambers Street. The distinctive Renaissance-style skyscraper, designed by Willam M. Kendall of McKim, Mead & White, is shown here shortly before its completion in 1914. The building's circular temple top would be crowned by Adolph A. Weinman's gilded statue, "Civic Pride." In front of the Municipal Building is the bold mansard roof of the Surrogate's Court—originally the Hall of Records— constructed between 1899 and 1911 from designs by John R. Thomas and Horgan & Slattery.*

LEFT: *With its fine limestone façade, dramatically tall roof, decorated dormers, and corner tower, the former home of Engine Company No. 31 of the New York City Fire Department is a veritable Loire château set down at the corner of Lafayette and White streets. Numerous elements of Napoleon LeBrun & Sons' 1895 creation echo those of Azay-le-Rideaux, a Renaissance château much admired by the École des Beaux-Arts.* ART COMMISSION.

OPPOSITE: *The gray granite U.S. Custom House at One Bowling Green, designed by Cass Gilbert and completed in 1907, is another Beaux Arts building in which sculpture is used to articulate its purpose. Here, Daniel Chester French's four sculptural groups representing the continents proclaim New York's commerce with the world. In this photograph, George B. Post's magnificent Produce Exchange of 1884 may be seen in the background. The Exchange was demolished in 1957.* LIBRARY OF CONGRESS.

· RICHMOND · BOROUGH · HALL ·
· ST·GEORGE · STATEN · ISLAND · N·Y·

CARRÈRE · HASTINGS
ARCHITECTS · NEW YORK

The Staten Island Borough Hall in St. George is one of the most original of all of New York's government buildings. Designed in 1904 by Carrère & Hastings, the handsome brick edifice, with its mansard roof, elegant limestone detailing, and big clock tower, is a flawless evocation of a 17th-century French Hotel de Ville. It is likely that John W. Carrère took a special interest in the project since he resided on Staten Island. ART COMMISSION.

EXCHANGE. CUSTOM HOUSE.

The New York Police Department Central Headquarters building at 240 Centre Street provides the passerby with an unexpected visual treat. Hoppin & Koen, who designed the building in 1909, used the unusual trapezoidal site to produce a Beaux Arts structure that gives Little Italy an unabashed example of civic grandeur. The baroque dome on its high column–encircled drum would not be out of place in Rome. In 1988 the Police Headquarters was converted to apartments.

PRIVATE COLLECTION.

OPPOSITE: Peter M. Coco's Queens County Court House of 1908 is a delightful example of the Beaux Arts embracing the Italian baroque. The bold use of varied materials—limestone, brick, and two tones of gray granite—the partially battered basement, the rich over-scaled consoles supporting the cornice, and the powerful paired Ionic columns flanking the entrance give the court house an architectural vibrancy of the type found in Rome or even Naples. This surprising civic structure, located on Long Island City's Court Square, now serves as a branch of the New York State Supreme Court.

QUEENS PUBLIC LIBRARY.

51

BELOW AND RIGHT: *When it was built in 1911, the First Precinct Police Headquarters at 100 Old Slip in Lower Manhattan was proclaimed New York's first modern police station. Its architects, Hunt & Hunt, sons of Richard Morris Hunt, composed a Renaissance mannerist masterpiece whose rusticated elevations give it an air of impregnability, the right note considering its function. The structure—seen at right in 1914—now serves as the headquarters of the New York Landmarks Preservation Commission.*

RIGHT: PRIVATE COLLECTION.
BELOW: ART COMMISSION.

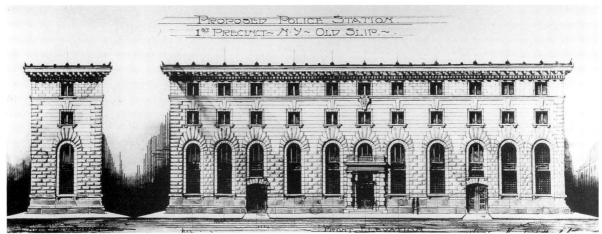

ABOVE: *The approach to the Manhattan Bridge, with its Bernini-like colonnade and triumphal arch, reveals Carrère & Hastings's attempt to bring the sense of a city gate to river-moated Manhattan. The central portal is a close copy of Paris's Port St.-Denis, erected in 1672. The approach, on Canal Street at the Bowery, was designed in 1910. In this 1917 photograph it is bedecked with patriotic motifs, inspired by the First World War.*
PRIVATE COLLECTION.

LEFT: *New York continued to construct stately civic buildings in the decades following the First World War. In 1912 Boston architect Guy Lowell won the competition for a New York County Court House, but the edifice was not completed until 1926, the year this photograph was taken. The sculptor of the figures in the pediment and on the roofline was Frederick Warren Allen, who taught sculpture at Harvard.*
PRIVATE COLLECTION.

Henry Siegel and his partner, Frank H. Cooper, were successful Chicago retail merchants who wanted to conquer New York. Conquer they did when, in 1896, their Siegel-Cooper & Company opened on Sixth Avenue between 18th and 19th streets. Designed by De Lemos & Cordes, the nearly block-square terra cotta–embellished structure contained more than fifteen acres of space on its nine sales floors. It resembled nothing so much as the private residence of a princely Roman family. The last vestiges of "The Big Store," as it was called, disappeared in 1918, but the building itself survives and is now part of the thriving Ladies' Mile Historic District.

Chapter Four

Commercial Grace

NEW YORK HAS ALWAYS BEEN A CITY OF merchants, traders, and manufacturers; its most august names have their beginnings in commerce. The Roosevelts were sugar refiners, the Schermerhorns were ship chandlers, the Rhinelanders bakers, the Goelets iron-mongers, the Astors fur traders, and the Guggenheims associated with mining and smelting. In its early days New York's businessmen made their impression on the city with banks and offices in the Greek Revival style, two- and three-story structures of brick and stone decorated with Doric, Ionic, and Corinthian columns and pilasters. Then came taller buildings, often of an Italianate style, and made of cast-iron, such as James Bogardus's Harper & Brothers printing plant on Pearl Street and John W. Kellum's A. T. Stewart department store on Broadway. But the Beaux Arts, with its use of the grandest modes of the past and its employment of the most modern building techniques and materials, empowered New York's businessmen to express their desires with an opulence and a scale previously unimaginable. In place of Paris's Palais de l'Élysée, Palais-Royal, and Palais du Luxembourg, New York presented to the world the exquisite glass- and iron-fronted Scribner's store, the elegant Chamber of Commerce, the Renaissance-inspired Herald Building, and the soaring Singer and Woolworth Towers. These edifices signified Gotham's ambitions and pride. These were the true palaces of its heart.

Henry Maillard's Retail Confectionary and Ladies Lunch Establishment in the Fifth Avenue Hotel, southwest corner of Broadway and 24th Street, is shown here in 1902. Maillard, a native of Normandy, manufactured his own chocolates and sold them in Belle-Epoque bonbonniers covered with a choice of artificial violets, lilies-of-the-valley, or rosebuds. The Fifth Avenue Hotel came down in 1908, and with it Maillard's Gilded Age shop.

PRIVATE COLLECTION.

BELOW, LEFT: *For his Charles Scribner's Sons Building on Fifth Avenue between 21st and 22nd streets, completed in 1894, Ernest Flagg combined a welcoming shopfront of iron and glass at street level, with space for the publishing house's* offices above. *The building is decorated for the 1910 homecoming of Theodore Roosevelt, a Scribner's author.* MUSEUM OF THE CITY OF NEW YORK.

BELOW, RIGHT: *Charles Scribner's Sons' 1902 publicity photograph of Edith Wharton. Scribner's was the publisher of Wharton's great New York novels,* The Age of Innocence *and* The House of Mirth. PRIVATE COLLECTION.

Few New York skyscrapers have as distinctive a profile as that of the Metropolitan Life Insurance Company on Madison Square. Completed in 1909, it is Napoleon LeBrun & Sons' 700-foot version of the campanile of Venice's San Marco. In the days before radio, the tower's lights announced election results: those on its south side signaled a Democratic victory, while those on the north indicated that the Republicans had won. This view down Madison Avenue shows the tower under construction. On the left is the tower of Madison Square Garden, loosely modeled on that of the Giralda in Seville.
PRIVATE COLLECTION.

OPPOSITE: *At the turn of the century R. H. Macy & Company migrated north from the 14th Street area to Herald Square. In this 1908 photograph, looking northwest at Broadway and 34th Street, the* handsome new Beaux Arts home that De Lemos & Cordes gave Macy's in 1902 may be seen looming over a corner holdout.
PRIVATE COLLECTION.

Perhaps the greatest loss among Beaux Arts commercial buildings was the distinguished art gallery and offices that René Sergent and Horace Trumbauer designed for Duveen Brothers at the northwest corner of Fifth Avenue and 56th Street. The building's deeply channeled base carried giant engaged Corinthian columns, while above the cornice rose a tall attic surmounted by a mansard roof. The structure, at once daring and irreproachably composed, was the perfect American headquarters for Joseph Duveen, the British purveyor of old masters to clients such as Henry Clay Frick and Collis P. Huntington. Designed in 1911, this masterwork of French taste was replaced in 1953 by one of Fifth Avenue's most banal edifices. DUVEEN BROTHERS.

LEFT: *The Singer Building, Broadway at Liberty Street, shows Ernest Flagg working in an exuberant French Renaissance style. Constructed in stages between 1897 and 1908, it was, at 612 feet, for a time the tallest building in the world. When it was demolished in the late 1960s, it was the tallest building ever torn down.*
PRIVATE COLLECTION.

ABOVE: *The architects and draftsmen of Ernest Flagg's office about the time of the First World War. The offices of Beaux Arts–trained architects, such as Flagg, were often imbued with the camaraderie their chiefs had known in their Paris ateliers.*
AVERY ARCHITECTURE AND FINE ARTS LIBRARY.

Among the most noble lobbies of any New York office tower is that of the American Telephone & Telegraph Building— begun in 1912—on Broadway between Dey and Fulton streets. Its architect, William Wells Bosworth, gave the building an entrance hall so populated with taffy-colored Doric columns that it seems to echo the pillared chambers of imperial Rome or pharaonic Egypt. The lobby's decorative elements are by Paul Manship and Gaston Lachaise.

61

OPPOSITE: *The advent in 1904 of Eidlitz & MacKenzie's Times Tower led to Long Acre Square being renamed Times Square. In the 1960s it was stripped of its sheath of pink granite and terra cotta. In this 1917 photograph, looking south from 46th Street, the former Olympia Theatre is on the left, with the Hotel Rector beyond, completed in 1911 by D. H. Burnham & Co. It succeeded the legendary Rector's Restaurant, which had stood on the site.* PRIVATE COLLECTION.

RIGHT: *It is rare for a New York structure to have as unusual a shape as the triangular Flatiron Building on Madison Square. Designed by Daniel Burnham, who was a key champion of Beaux Arts architecture at the 1893 World's Fair, the Renaissance-ornamented skyscraper resembles a tall ship sailing up Fifth Avenue. Here it is seen in a charcoal and ink wash by Jules Guerin in 1902, the year it was completed.* THE ART INSTITUTE OF CHICAGO.

63

LEFT AND BELOW: *Though Beaux Arts architects seldom designed in the Gothic mode, Frank Woolworth, father of the "Five-and-Ten," insisted on that style for his 1913 "Cathedral of Commerce" at Broadway and Barclay Street. His ideal was London's Houses of Parliament. Woolworth's architect, Cass Gilbert, produced a soaring 729-foot terra cotta–clad Gothic tower that is undoubtedly one of the world's most beautiful skyscrapers.* PRIVATE COLLECTIONS.

OPPOSITE: *Richard Upjohn's Gothic Revival Trinity Church at Broadway and Wall Street of 1846 is hemmed in by Beaux Arts behemoths in this 1916 photograph. Left to right, the limestone Trinity Building by Francis H. Kimball, 1908; the massive 4l-story Equitable Building by Ernest R. Graham, 1915; the 22-story granite American Surety Building by Bruce Price, 1895; and the 12-story pyramid-topped Bankers Trust Company by Trowbridge & Livingston, 1912. The Equitable's astounding 1.2 million square feet of space on a less than one-acre site led in 1916 to new zoning laws.* LIBRARY OF CONGRESS.

One of Brooklyn's outstanding Beaux Arts commercial buildings was the Brooklyn Savings Bank at the northeast corner of Pierrepont and Clinton streets. Completed in 1894, the bank's triumphal arch entrance and impressive banking room, surmounted by an oblong dome, showed the influence of the 1893 Chicago World's Fair. But there was also an element in this extraordinary structure by the Canadian-born Frank Freeman reminiscent of the compositions of English baroque architects such as Nicholas Hawksmoor. The Brooklyn Savings Bank was a victim of urban renewal in the 1960s. BROOKLYN HISTORICAL SOCIETY.

ABOVE, LEFT: *Despite the restrictions of its site, George B. Post achieved a sumptuous monumentality for the New York Stock Exchange on Broad Street, completed in 1903.*

The façade is a vibrant composition of marble balconies, giant Corinthian columns, and a pediment alive with John Quincy Adams Ward's "Integrity Protecting the Works of Man." The restrained headquarters of J. P. Morgan & Company—Trowbridge & Livingston, 1913—may be seen to the left. LIBRARY OF CONGRESS.

ABOVE, RIGHT: *The floor of the Exchange in 1908. The uniformed young men at one of the "Posts" where stocks were sold are pages.* LIBRARY OF CONGRESS.

OPPOSITE: *One of the city's little-known Beaux Arts masterpieces is James B. Baker's white marble Chamber of Commerce of 1901 on Liberty Street. The glory of the build-ing—the sculptural groups by Philip Martiny and Daniel Chester French, and the Mercury by Karl Bitter— have all disappeared.* CHAMBER OF COMMERCE.

ABOVE: *The Great Hall of the Chamber of Commerce was lined with imposing por-traits of leading figures in the history of American business. The building has been sold and was recently a dress shop.* CHAMBER OF COMMERCE.

The most beautiful façade of any theater in the Broadway area belongs to the Lyceum on West 45th Street. Designed by the great theater architectural team of Herts & Tallant, the Beaux Arts Lyceum was built by the famed impresario Daniel Frohman and opened in 1903 with Ethel Barrymore in Cousin Kate. The intimate house, with its handsome murals by James Wall Finn, has, in the words of the critic Brooks Atkinson, "the warmth and hospitality of a cordial era." NEW-YORK HISTORICAL SOCIETY.

Chapter Five

Public Pleasures

IN HIS 1900 NOVEL, *Sister Carrie*, Theodore Dreiser has his heroine stroll down Broadway: "The walk down Broadway, then as now, was one of the remarkable features of the city. It was a very imposing procession of pretty faces and fine clothes. Women appeared in their very best hats, shoes, and gloves and walked arm in arm on their way to the fine shops or theatres strung along from Fourteenth to Thirty-fourth streets." What Dreiser has captured is the extraordinary public life of New York at the turn of the century.

With the new electric street cars facilitating movement and the new electric lights banishing night, New Yorkers flocked to places of entertainment and stayed up late as never before. It was the era when serious dinner parties began after the opera, when formal balls started at midnight, when, in the summer, roof gardens, like those atop Madison Square Garden and the Astor Hotel, were thronged all night long by middle-class New Yorkers attempting to escape the heat in the days before air conditioning.

This was also the era when a rapidly growing city developed a taste for gargantuan dining establishments like the new five-story Delmonico's that opened at the northeast corner of Fifth Avenue and 44th Street in 1897. Delmonico's boasted no less than forty-three cooks, but it faced keen competition from the new nearby Sherry's, which offered "table de luxe" dinners for $3.00. With Paris's Opera House and its dazzling restaurants like the Ritz Hotel's dining room, New York's Beaux Arts architects had no difficulty providing the appropriate mise-en-scène for any festivity. Looking at photographs of their vanished pleasure domes—spaces such as Carrère & Hastings's Metropolitan Opera House auditorium or Stanford White's Sherry's ballroom—one can almost hear the rustle of satin and the strains of a Victor Herbert melody, perhaps the "Gypsy Love Song" from his 1898 hit, *The Fortune Teller*:

> *Slumber on, my little gypsy sweetheart,*
> *Dream of the field and the grove;*
> *Can you hear me, hear me in that dreamland*
> *Where your fancies rove?*

In their settings for public pleasures, the Beaux Arts architects proved that, long before Disney, they were indeed creators of dreamlands.

The 1,200-seat Garden Theatre opened on September 28, 1890, with the English comedy Doctor Bill. Its interior, with striped silk hangings and a color scheme of cream, white, and gold, received universal praise, as did its painted curtain, a copy of Boldini's "The Park at Versailles." White, a devotee of the stage, insisted that the Garden Theatre have the most up-to-date stage equipment available.
PRIVATE COLLECTION.

When Madison Square Garden, filling the entire block bounded by Madison and Fourth avenues and 26th and 27th streets, opened its vast 10,000-seat amphitheatre in the spring of 1890, it instantly made Stanford White the most famous architect in New York. The yellow brick and terra cotta edifice also held a 1,500-seat concert hall and a theater and was topped by a tower rising 341 feet from the pavement. The tower contained seven floors of apartments and was crowned by Augustus Saint-Gaudens's graceful 13-foot statue of Diana. Following the Garden's demolition in 1925, Diana went to the Philadelphia Museum of Art. MUSEUM OF THE CITY OF NEW YORK.

74

LEFT: *The Delmonico family had steadily moved their establishments up Manhattan since opening their first on William Street in 1827. Delmonico's final incarnation was the limestone Renaissance palazzo capped by electric lights James Brown Lord designed for it at the northeast corner of Fifth Avenue and 44th Street. It is seen here on the right shortly after its opening in November of 1897. Across the Avenue is the multi-corniced façade of its arch rival, Sherry's. The culinary shrine served its last lobster in May of 1923 and fell to the wrecking ball two years later.* PRIVATE COLLECTION.

ABOVE, RIGHT: *Built by the great theatrical promoter, Oscar Hammerstein, the Olympia Theatre, designed by John B. McElfatrick, occupied the entire block on the east side of Broadway between 44th and 45th streets. When it opened in November of 1895, it was seen to be an entertainment complex of luxurious Beaux Arts interiors, including the Louis XIV–style*

Music Hall, the Louis XV–style Concert Hall, and the Louis XVI–style Lyric Theatre. Within three years Hammerstein was so deeply in debt that the Olympia was sold at auction. It was reorganized as three separate theaters, The Lyric, The Roof Garden, and The Music Hall, which became the New York Theatre. The astonishing structure came down in 1935 and was replaced by the Criterion movie house.* NEW-YORK HISTORICAL SOCIETY.

BELOW, RIGHT: *From her New York debut at Booth's Theatre in 1880 until her final appearance in the city at the Brooklyn Academy of Music in 1918, the matchless French tragedienne, Sarah Bernhardt, was one of Beaux Arts New York's most popular actresses. In this 1896 photograph, "The Divine Sarah" poses in her suite at the Hoffman House, a hotel on Broadway between 24th and 25th streets much favored by theatrical people.* PRIVATE COLLECTION.

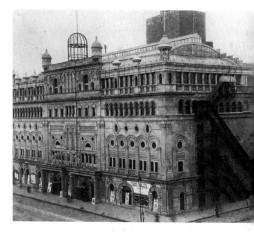

Beginning in the 1880s, New York witnessed an efflorescence of public roof gardens made accessible and popular by the new elevators and increasing height of buildings that afforded dazzling views of the city. The roof gardens atop Madison Square Garden and the Astor Hotel were but two of the most famous. The garden atop the American Theatre at the southeast corner of Eighth Avenue and 42nd Street— seen here in 1898—offered not only a refreshing way to escape the summer heat, but a full vaudeville bill as well. MUSEUM OF THE CITY OF NEW YORK.

The receptivity of Beaux Arts architects to past styles permitted them to create sensational fantasy interiors for theaters and restaurants. Among the latter, one of the most memorable was Murray's Roman Gardens on West 42nd Street, designed by Henry Erkins in 1907. The main dining room was a free interpretation of the atrium of a Pompeian villa, replete with columns and caryatids. PRIVATE COLLECTION.

A dazzling example of what Beaux Arts architects could do with a narrow site is Herts & Tallant's New Amsterdam Theatre of 1903. The theater's 42nd Street façade featured a high, welcoming entrance flanked by handsome lamp stanchions, a window with French Art Nouveau elements, topped by a horseshoe arch bearing statues representing music, drama, and comedy by George Gray Barnard and Hinton Perry. The New Amsterdam, which opened with a Klaw and Erlanger production of A Midsummer Night's Dream that starred Nat Goodwin, became, in 1913, the home of the legendary Ziegfeld Follies. After serving as a movie palace, the remarkable theater is once again a legitimate house. NEW-YORK HISTORICAL SOCIETY.

BELOW: *Between 1903 and 1904, following a fire, Carrère & Hastings transformed the Metropolitan Opera House's auditorium into a luminescent maroon and gold Beaux Arts chamber with the tiers of seats sweeping in great arcs from the handsome proscenium. This was the house of Toscanini, Lehmann, and Caruso.* PRIVATE COLLECTION.

The dour exterior Josiah Cleveland Cady gave the Metropolitan Opera House, which opened in 1863, earned it the epithet "The Yellow Brick Brewery." Dour would most certainly not describe the patrons— including Vanderbilts and Goulds—who built the new house to supplant the old Academy of Music on 14th Street where they had been denied boxes. The old Metropolitan, located on Broadway between 39th and 40th streets, was razed in 1957. METROPOLITAN OPERA ARCHIVES.

Coney Island's Luna Park, which opened in 1903, was the creation of theatrical promoter Frederick Thompson. It was influenced by both the 1893 Chicago World's Fair and the White City, an amusement park on Chicago's south side that flourished through the 1920s. Luna Park's fantastic wood and plaster towers, arches, and domes—outlined by electric lights at night—show how broad was the appeal of certain elements of the Beaux Arts style.

PRIVATE COLLECTION.

New York's lambent Beaux
Arts elegance just before the
First World War is captured in
this 1914 photograph of a
young woman leaning against
the balustrade of the terrace of
the New York Public Library.
A bronze lamp, designed by
Carrère & Hastings, glows
near her, while at the right
may be seen the silhouette of
the fabulous base of Thomas
Hastings's flagpole cast by
Tiffany Studios. AMERICAN
ARCHITECTURAL ARCHIVES.

Chapter Six

Celebrating Art and Learning

NEW YORK, COMPARED TO OTHER GREAT CITIES such as Paris and London, labors under a serious handicap. Although it had been the nation's capital in 1789 and 1790, it had seen the government move first to Philadelphia and then to Washington. New Yorkers were stung when, after a visit in 1888, the distinguished English jurist, Lord James Brice, commented: "New York, which has as little a claim to be the social or intellectual as to be the political capital of the country, is emphatically, its financial capital." For rich New Yorkers that was not enough. In the Gilded Age, they self-consciously set out to make the city America's cultural capital. Extraordinary collectors, such as James Lenox, J. Pierpont Morgan, and Henry Clay Frick were determined to create libraries and art collections that would be the equal of any in the world. All knew that to achieve this goal the structures housing their collections must have a sense of monumentality, and this was effectively supplied by that most monumental of styles, the Beaux Arts. Thus they could emulate the edifices that housed the great collections abroad—the Louvre in Paris, the Villa Medici in Rome, the Pitti Palace in Florence. Fortunately, they chose their architects well: Lenox with Richard Morris Hunt, Morgan with Charles F. McKim, and Frick with Carrère & Hastings. Their example was followed by those responsible for building almost all of New York's public halls of art and learning. Daniel Burnham, the Chicago architect who promoted the Beaux Arts for that city's 1893

Columbian Exposition and who designed New York's Flatiron Building, stated: "Make no little plans; they have no magic to stir men's blood. . . . Make big plans; aim high in hope and work. Let your watchword be order and your beacon beauty." The New York Public Library and the Metropolitan Museum of Art, Low Library at Columbia and The Frick Collection, the Brooklyn Museum of Art and the Morgan Library, among many other New York institutions, celebrate art and learning with Beaux-Arts edifices imbued with order and beauty and magic.

RIGHT: *Construction in progress on the entrance of the New York Public Library. Following guidelines set by the Library's first director, John S. Billings, a design competition was announced in May of 1897. Carrère & Hastings won over a large field that included McKim, Mead & White and George B. Post. The façade is a brilliant interpretation of that combination of monumentality and refinement found in 18th-century French architecture as exemplified by Gabriel's twin palaces on the north side of the Place de la Concorde. This was no coincidence, for Carrère wrote that these had been produced in architecture's "last great historical period."* NEW YORK PUBLIC LIBRARY.

BELOW, LEFT: *Modelers at work on a Corinthian capital in the model room of the unfinished New York Public Library. To ensure perfection, Carrère & Hastings had scale models made of everything from doorways to stair railings. The plaster of Paris model of the library itself was commissioned by the trustees and displayed at various locations—including City Hall— to win public support for a building of the finest materials. The campaign worked, and instead of being constructed of brick—as had first been suggested—the library was made of crystalline marble.* NEW YORK PUBLIC LIBRARY.

COPYRIGHT 1917 BY
AMERICAN STUDIO N.Y.

Carrère & Hastings's white
Dorset, Vermont, marble
palace for the New York Public
Library at Fifth Avenue and
42nd Street is one of the city's
premier examples of Beaux
Arts beauty and panache.
The Library was formed in
1895 through the merging of
the Astor Library, the Lenox
Library, and the Tilden Trust,
and its building was completed
in 1911. Just beyond the
Library in this 1917 view looking south is the very Parisian
mansarded structure that John
H. Duncan designed in 1902
for the Knox Hat Company.

ABOVE, LEFT: *Richard Morris Hunt's Lenox Library, completed in 1875 on Fifth Avenue between 70th and 71st streets, was constructed to house the book and art collection of real estate magnate James P. Lenox. The building—with its use of fine materials such as bronze and varied colored marbles and masterfully composed classical elements—was one of New York's first structures to reveal the powerful monumentality Beaux Arts design could bring to the urban scene. The Library—seen here in 1905—was demolished in 1912 to make way for the Frick Collection.* PRIVATE COLLECTION.

ABOVE, RIGHT: *The Frick Collection is a precious survivor of the era when Fifth Avenue was lined with Beaux Arts residences. Constructed between 1911 and 1914 by Thomas Hastings of Carrère & Hastings for Mr. and Mrs. Henry Clay Frick, it is a stunning example of 18th-century French architectural ideas carried to Manhattan. Its interiors—such as the Fragonard Room—were designed by Sir Charles Allom of White Allom, London.* COPYRIGHT THE FRICK COLLECTION, PHOTOGRAPH BY JOHN BIGELOW TAYLOR.

BELOW AND OPPOSITE: *Charles F. McKim began designing the Pierpont Morgan Library at 33 East 36th Street for financier John Pierpont Morgan in 1902. When it was completed in 1906, the comparatively small structure had cost $1.2 million. The East Room, built to hold Morgan's collection of rare books, was decorated by the painter H. Siddons Mowbray. The 16th-century Brussels tapestry above the mantlepiece, also 16th century, depicts Avarice, one of the Seven Deadly Sins.*

The exterior of the Library, of marble laid in the Greek manner without mortar, borrows design elements from the garden casinos that proliferated in Italy in the Renaissance. THE PIERPONT MORGAN LIBRARY. PHOTOGRAPH BY TODD EBERLE.

BELOW: *Only one-quarter of McKim, Mead & White's 1897 grand plan for the Brooklyn Institute of Arts and Sciences (now the Brooklyn Museum of Art) was carried out, but even that fragment was spectacular. Alas, the Eastern Parkway entrance has been shorn of its ceremonial flight of stairs. Daniel Chester French was in charge of the sculpture for the pediment, while the statues decorating the wings are by, among others, Karl Bitter, Kenyon Cox, Edward C. Potter, and Janet Scudder.*
BROOKLYN PUBLIC LIBRARY.

BELOW, LEFT: *The Metropolitan Museum of Art's Fifth Avenue façade is one of America's supreme Beaux Arts compositions. The central pavilion, by Richard Morris Hunt and his son, Richard Howland Hunt, was completed in 1902, a year before this photograph was taken. The massive blocks of stone atop the Museum's paired Corinthian columns were intended to be carved into figural groups representing the four great periods of art: Egyptian, Greek, Renaissance, and Modern. They are still unfinished.*
PRIVATE COLLECTION.

The Metropolitan Museum's Great Hall—166 feet long and 48 feet wide—rises to three high saucer-shaped domes that echo the façade's triple arches. This imperial limestone chamber was originally intended to display the Museum's cast collection.

THE PRINTS AND DRAWINGS COLLECTION, THE OCTAGON, WASHINGTON, D.C.

St. Luke's Hospital, a center of medical education and healing, opened its new building on Morningside Drive between 113th and 114th streets in 1896. Designed by Ernest Flagg, the hospital was one of the city's most ambitious Beaux Arts structures and was crowned by a baroque dome that would have been at home in Prague. In the 1960s, the hospital's western pavilions were demolished and its spectacular dome shaved off. PHOTOGRAPH BY ESTHER BUBLEY.

The Gould Library, named for financier Jay Gould, was the focus of New York University's Bronx campus situated on a ridge above the Harlem River. Construction of the yellow brick and terra-cotta edifice, reminiscent of both the Pantheon in Rome and Andrea Palladio's Villa Rotunda near Venice, began in 1896. The library's architect, Stanford White, gave it an elegant Corinthian portico. New York University sold its uptown campus in 1973 and the Gould Library now serves Bronx Community College. PRIVATE COLLECTION.

When, in the 1890s, the commissions for the new campuses of both Columbia University and New York University came into the McKim, Mead & White office, the jobs were split. McKim took charge of Columbia's new Morningside Heights campus, while White chose—perhaps because it was his father's alma mater— to work on New York University's new Bronx campus. Both architects made the library the center of their academic plan. McKim's Low Memorial Library was made possible by a gift of $1 million from Columbia president Seth Low, and named in honor of his father, Abiel Abbot Low. McKim's gray stone building, with its screen of fluted Ionic columns supporting a massive rectangular attic and crowned by a dome echoing that of the Pantheon in Rome, brought to the Columbia campus a majestic monumentality. Low Memorial Library was but seven years old when this photograph, looking northwest at 116th Street and Amsterdam Avenue, was made in 1905. On the right are Schermerhorn and Fayerweather Halls, also designed by McKim.

Chapter Seven

Places of Worship and Urban Monuments

IF THERE WAS ANY STYLE other than the classical that Beaux Arts architects respected, it was the Gothic. But after a series of heated debates in the 1860s, the École des Beaux-Arts rejected the Gothic as the supreme style. For New York's Beaux Arts architects, working in a city where such ecclesiastical landmarks as Trinity Church and St. Patrick's Cathedral were designed in the Gothic style, this presented a challenge. Yet it was merely a challenge to be overcome. Typically, when some of the congregation of the Madison Square Presbyterian Church objected to Stanford White's proposal to build them a classical sanctuary rather than one in the expected Gothic style, White told them that Presbyterians are Protestants and "have no affiliations whatsoever with Gothic. Gothic . . . belongs absolutely and only to the Roman Catholic Church." Of course, when White redecorated the chancel of the Roman Catholic Church of St. Paul the Apostle on Columbus Avenue, his high altar recalled the classicism of Rome's Santa Maria Maggiore. The happy result of this fast footwork was that New York was blessed with the soaring campanile of Judson Memorial Church in Greenwich Village, the splendid Renaissance-inspired chancel of the Church of the Ascension on Lower Fifth Avenue, and the radiant portals of St. Bartholomew's Church now on Park Avenue.

Stanford White's Judson Memorial Church of 1893 on Washington Square South is a flawless composition of Romanesque and Renaissance Italian design themes carried out in thin, yellow Roman brick and cream-colored terra cotta. Judson's noble doorway, flanked by Corinthian columns and covered by a crisp hood topped by an anthemion, recalls the entrances to Venetian churches. NEW-YORK HISTORICAL SOCIETY.

93

ABOVE: *One of New York's most lamented lost places of worship is the Madison Square Presbyterian Church, which stood at the northeast corner of Madison Avenue and 24th Street. Dedicated in 1906, the church echoed Thomas Jefferson's Rotunda at the University of Virginia which its architect, Stanford White, had recently restored after a fire. Its portico was particularly notable, consisting of six 30-foot pale green Corinthian columns supporting a pediment filled with cream and blue terra cotta reliefs by Adolph A. Weinman and H. Siddons Mowbray. This gem of a building was swept away in 1919 to make room for the expansion of the Metropolitan Life Insurance Company.*
PRIVATE COLLECTION.

If there was a tendency in America in the 19th century to design houses of worship in the Gothic style, this was most certainly not the case when it came to public monuments. The fact that the capitol in Washington was classical had a good deal to do with this. The Beaux Arts architects' desire to embellish New York with noble public monuments sprang from their wish to make Gotham as glorious as Paris and Rome, and also from the City Beautiful movement, which envisioned metropolises of grand boulevards studded with heroic statues, obelisks, and triumphal arches. That astute critic, Henry James, after a visit to New York in 1905, acknowledged just how often these dreams became reality. Looking at the Sherman monument near Central Park, he wrote: "The best thing in the picture, obviously, is Saint-Gaudens's great group, splendid in its golden elegance. . . ." James was not one to use either "splendid" or "great" lightly.

OPPOSITE, BELOW: *The death in 1899 of Cornelius Vanderbilt II led to the commissioning of Stanford White to create a portal in his honor for the old St. Bartholomew's Church at Madison Avenue and 44th Street. Completed in 1902, in 1917 the portal was moved to the new St. Bartholomew's on Park Avenue. Inspired by the* 12th-century abbey in the French village of St.-Gilles-du-Gard, the portal, with its superb sculpture by Herbert Adams, Daniel Chester French, Andrew O'Conner, and Philip Martiny, was called by critic Royal Cortissoz "the most noble work of its kind in modern times." PRIVATE COLLECTION.

LEFT: *One of the most astonishing sanctuaries in New York is the First Church of Christ Scientist at 1 West 96th Street. With its bold massing, freely used classical elements, and stone spire rising unexpectedly from a square tower embellished with urns, this granite Beaux Arts edifice recalls the surprising churches of English architects like Hawksmoor and George Steuart. Designed by Carrère & Hastings, the First Church was completed in 1903.* LIBRARY OF CONGRESS.

ABOVE: *The interior of the First Church strikingly expresses the presence of the arching steel girders that frame the structure while humanizing them with robust plaster rosettes, garlands, and molding. It is an unforgettable example of how Beaux Arts architects embraced the products of the factory without making the factory itself their aesthetic prototype.* LIBRARY OF CONGRESS.

OPPOSITE: *Congregation Shearith Israel, the historic Spanish and Portuguese synagogue, was founded in 1654. It is the oldest Jewish congregation in North America. The congregation's present home, at Central Park West and 70th Street, is a nobly composed classical building by the distinguished Beaux Arts architect, Arnold Brunner, who completed it in 1897.* CONGREGATION SHEARITH ISRAEL.

ABOVE, LEFT: *The Beaux Arts ideal that architects and artists should work together to create a new Renaissance, an American Renaissance, is exemplified by the cooperative effort that took place in 1887 in the chancel of the Roman Catholic Church of St. Paul the Apostle on Columbus Avenue and 59th Street. St. Paul's has stained glass windows by John La Farge, a hanging sanctuary lamp by Philip Martiny, and a high altar by Stanford White, whose magnificent baldachino is adorned with angels by Frederick MacMonnies. Alas, liturgical changes have led to the construction of a pedestrian modern altar in front of White's glorious one.* THE PAULIST FATHERS.

ABOVE, RIGHT: *The only Beaux Arts chapel among the seven in the awesome Episcopal Cathedral of St. John the Divine on Morningside Heights is that of St. Ambrose designed by Carrère & Hastings. That it was not in the Gothic style embraced by the Cathedral's architect of the time, Ralph Adams Cram, was due to the insistence of its patron, Sara Whiting Rives. As is appropriate in a chapel celebrating Christianity in Italy, every element, including the floor of Siena, Verona, and Cenere marbles, the walls of Rosato, and the windows by Henry Wynd Young, reverberates with Italian Renaissance motifs. Particularly fine is the alabaster altar with its early Renaissance–style gilded reredos. St. Ambrose was dedicated in April of 1914.* THE CATHEDRAL OF ST. JOHN THE DIVINE.

With the famed arches of Rome and Paris in mind, Beaux Arts architects used the form to bring beauty and a sense of history to the streets of New York. Generally constructed of inexpensive perishable materials—wood and staff, a plaster stiffened with hemp fibers—it was hoped that their beauty would result in funds being found to reconstruct the arches in stone. The most astounding of these temporary arches was the one raised on Fifth Avenue north of 23rd Street in 1899 to honor Admiral George Dewey. Twenty-eight of America's leading sculptors contributed to its decoration. In this view looking north, the "Victory Upon the Sea" group atop the arch is by J. Q. A. Ward, while "The Combat" on the right pier is by Karl Bitter. The dapper gentleman in the foreground is the architect, Charles R. Lamb. COURTESY OF BAREA LAMB SEELEY.

In this view looking south, "Victory" by Herbert Adams seems to spring from one of the columns flanking the arch to crown the hero of Manila Bay. On the pier in the background is "Peace" by Daniel Chester French. The admiral passed under his arch in the great homecoming parade New York held in his honor on September 30, 1899. It was expected that the widely praised monument would be made permanent, but Dewey, after making some impolitic remarks, quickly fell out of favor and his triumphal arch was dismantled in November, 1900. COURTESY OF BAREA LAMB SEELEY.

ABOVE AND RIGHT: *Stanford White was asked to design a temporary arch to commemorate the centennial in 1889 of George Washington's inauguration as first President of the United States. That arch—of wood and plaster—spanned Fifth Avenue some 150 feet north of Washington Square. The marble arch—* *also by White—was completed in 1895. The statue of Washington as "First in peace" on the arch's right side is by Alexander Stirling Calder, father of Alexander Calder. The winged figures in the spandrels are by Frederick MacMonnies.* NEW-YORK HISTORICAL SOCIETY; PRIVATE COLLECTION.

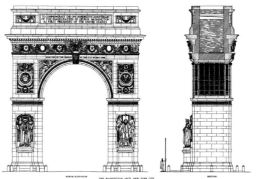

BELOW, LEFT: *If New York has an equivalent of Paris's Arc de Triomphe, it is undoubtedly the Soldiers' and Sailors' Memorial Arch* at the center of Brooklyn's Grand Army Plaza. Designed by John H. Duncan, it was completed in 1892. The spectacular quadriga that tops it and the groups representing the Army and Navy on the arch's south face are by Frederick MacMonnies. PRIVATE COLLECTION.

BELOW, RIGHT: *As the 400th anniversary of Columbus's first voyage to the New World approached, New York fought to win the right to host the national exposition planned to mark the event. It lost to Chicago, but nevertheless went ahead with its own celebrations. A city-sponsored design competition was held for a temporary arch to honor Columbus. The winner was Harry Hertz of Columbia University; his arch, patterned on that of Constantine in Rome, ornamented Fifth Avenue near Central Park. Thousands marched beneath it during the parades held on October 10th and 12th of* 1892. PRIVATE COLLECTION.

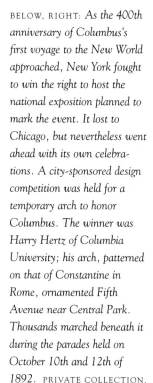

A legacy of the 1892 Columbus quatrecentenary celebrations is the 26-foot-high granite column, adorned with the bronze prows of ancient warships and topped by the explorer himself in marble by Gaetano Russo. In this 1910 photograph of Columbus Circle, the twin Gothic towers of the Church of St. Paul the Apostle stand out against the city's low skyline. NEW-YORK HISTORICAL SOCIETY.

BELOW: *The story of the 21-year-old American, Nathan Hale, being hanged as a spy by the British in New York in September, 1775, is one of the most moving episodes of the Revolution. Frederick MacMonnies was only 26 when he sculpted the young prisoner as he imagined he looked just before his execution. Located in City Hall Park, the poignant bronze standing upon a columnar granite base by Stanford White was unveiled in 1893.*
PRIVATE COLLECTION.

ABOVE: *The death of Ulysses S. Grant in 1885 led to an outpouring of grief for the President and Civil War general. More than 90,000 people—many of them black—paid for his granite Beaux Arts mausoleum on Riverside Drive at 122nd Street. While the exterior owes something to the Mausoleum of Halicarnassus, the interior owes everything to Napoleon's tomb in Paris. Architect John H. Duncan planned a grand sculptural program for the structure, but no more was added than is shown in this 1899 photograph, made two years after the tomb was completed.*
LIBRARY OF CONGRESS.

102

Among New York's most moving Beaux Arts memorials is the Prison Ship Martyrs' Monument in Brooklyn's Fort Greene Park, completed in 1909. Stanford White's 143-foot-tall Doric column bearing a bronze brazier by Adolph A. Weinman commemorates the 11,000 Americans who perished during the Revolution in the holds of British prison ships in Wallabout Bay. NEW-YORK HISTORICAL SOCIETY.

BELOW: *Based on Athens's Choragic Monument of Lysicrates, the Soldiers' and Sailors' Memorial on Riverside Drive at 89th Street, dedicated in 1902, is one of New York's numerous Civil War monuments. Its overall form is the work of Stoughton & Stoughton, while the decorative sculpture, such as the eagles above the cornice, are by Paul E. M. DuBoy.* LIBRARY OF CONGRESS.

This 1904 view looking north on Fifth Avenue shows Trowbridge & Livingston's luxurious new St. Regis Hotel in the distance. The handsome structure on 51st Street just north of St. Patrick's Cathedral is the Union Club, New York's oldest social club. Feeling the need to migrate north, the Union had abandoned its former home on Fifth Avenue at 21st Street and commissioned Cass Gilbert and John du Fais to build this Italian Renaissance clubhouse. The club moved in 1903 and exactly thirty years later migrated again to its present home on the northeast corner of Park Avenue and 69th Street.
PRIVATE COLLECTION.

Chapter Eight

Clubland

THE WIDESPREAD PROSPERITY OF AMERICA in the late 19th century was reflected in the growth of men's clubs as places for dining, entertainment, and important deal-making. Boston had its Somerset Club, Philadelphia its Union League, and Chicago its Chicago Club. The growth of clubs in New York, though, was particularly spectacular, with the number reaching an astounding 157 in 1901, with some 38,000 members. An important factor spurring this growth was a determination on the part of businessmen and others to emulate the exclusive men's clubs they had visited in London. Whereas in their early days clubs had inhabited rooms that they owned or rented in houses or in office buildings, the urge to impress and to expand soon led to exuberant Beaux Arts clubhouses. Among the most spectacular were the Metropolitan Club, designed by Stanford White at the northeast corner of 60th Street and Fifth Avenue, and the New York Yacht Club on West 44th Street by Whitney Warren. The opulence of these clubs and the free-spending ways of their members gave rise to one of Gilded-Age New York's most famous stories. As the tale is told, two actresses were having lunch one day at Delmonico's. "You know, I found a pearl in an oyster the other night at Rector's," the first actress announces. "Oh, that's nothing, my dear," the second actress responds. "Last night I got a diamond necklace off an old lobster at the Metropolitan Club."

The University Club, at
the northwest corner of Fifth
Avenue and 54th Street,
is Charles F. McKim's essay
in designing a Medicean
palazzo. Completed in 1899,
the pink granite clubhouse
advertises its raison d'être by
the marble seals of the colleges
and universities—the work
of Daniel Chester French—
that adorn its façade. In
this turn-of-the-century
photograph, the clubhouse
had not yet lost its granite
railings to the widening of
Fifth Avenue.

106

The Century Association, a club founded in 1847 for artists and men of letters, decided in 1889 to move from East 15th Street uptown to West 43rd Street just off Fifth Avenue. For the Century's new clubhouse Stanford White designed a dazzling façade of stone, brick, and terra cotta based on a 16th-century palazzo in Verona. The Century moved into its new home in 1891 and still resides there. NEW-YORK HISTORICAL SOCIETY.

The art gallery and library are the heart of the Century clubhouse. In his design of the library, White was aided by Francis L. V. Hoppin, who would later be the architect of the Mount, Edith Wharton's house in Lenox, Massachusetts. The high coved ceiling was gold leafed. THE CENTURY ASSOCIATION.

ABOVE, LEFT: *No New York clubhouse more perfectly expresses Beaux Arts élan than does Whitney Warren's New York Yacht Club on West 44th Street, seen here in 1901, the year it was complet-* ed. A delightful and appropri- *ate feature of its French Renaissance façade are the three bay windows fashioned after those on the stern of 17th-century Dutch vessels.* THE NEW YORK YACHT CLUB.

ABOVE, RIGHT: *By his use of colored marble columns crowned with exaggerated capitals, flamboyantly carved balustrades and banisters, and a high sweep of stairs, Whitney Warren succeeded* in giving to the Yacht Club's *entrance hall an imposing dignity equal to that of any London gentleman's club.* THE NEW YORK YACHT CLUB.

The New York Yacht Club's
Palm Cafe brought to West
44th Street the ambiance
of Europe's Palace Hotels,
such as the Hôtel de Paris in
Monte Carlo. Its glass and
iron dome originally admitted
natural light.

THE NEW YORK YACHT CLUB.

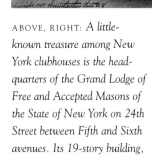

ABOVE, LEFT: *One of the oldest social clubs in New York is the Harmonie, whose origins go back to 1852 when it was founded as an exclusive German-Jewish organization under the name "Gesellschaft Harmonie." Stanford White's restrained clubhouse for "Our Crowd" at 4 East 60th Street opened in 1906.*

THE HARMONIE CLUB.

ABOVE, RIGHT: *A little-known treasure among New York clubhouses is the head-quarters of the Grand Lodge of Free and Accepted Masons of the State of New York on 24th Street between Fifth and Sixth avenues. Its 19-story building,* designed by Harry Percy Knowles and completed in 1909, houses a Grand Lodge Room and eleven other lodge rooms. Among them is the Renaissance Room, seen here the year it was completed. Furnished by the celebrated firm of Pottier & Stymus, the room is a resplendent Beaux Arts chamber of reeded Corinthian pilasters, gold and silver leaf, faux marble panels, and crystal chandeliers. LIBRARY OF CONGRESS.

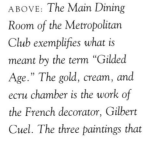

Chapter Nine

Domestic Opulence

WITH ITS TRIUMPH IN THE CIVIL WAR OVER the agrarian aristocracy of the South, the new industrialism of the North entered upon an era of unprecedented prosperity. Nowhere was this more evident than in New York, where the local new rich—Belmonts, Vanderbilts, and Whitneys—were soon joined by the new rich of the West—Fricks, Carnegies, and Millses. Abashed Knickerbocker New Yorkers referred to this onslaught as "The Gold Rush." One of the major opportunities and tests of the Beaux Arts architects was to design appropriate dwellings for the new American Medicis, houses that would be opulent, but not vulgar. The preceding fashionable styles of gloomy Romanesque, spindly Second Empire, and picturesque Queen Anne would not do. The correct note was sounded on the evening of March 22, 1883, when the gleaming French château Richard Morris Hunt had designed for Alva Vanderbilt at Fifth Avenue and 52nd Street was opened for Society's admiration. From now on the materials of which New York's mansions were built would be gleaming marble, glittering limestone, and bright yellow brick. The design precedents would be French or Italian, a castle

The brick and limestone New York version of Francois I's Fontainebleau built by Cornelius Vanderbilt II—a grandson of the Commodore and father of Gertrude Vanderbilt Whitney—was the largest private city house ever constructed in America. The first part of the mansion, at the northwest corner of Fifth Avenue and 57th Street, was completed in 1882 from designs by George B. Post. In 1892 Post—with the help of Richard Morris Hunt—extended the house to 58th Street and increased its size to 137 rooms. The mansion had stained glass by John La Farge, a superb mantelpiece by Saint-Gaudens—now in the Metropolitan Museum of Art—and a wonderful ceiling by Paul Baudry. It vanished in 1927 to be replaced by Bergdorf-Goodman. PRIVATE COLLECTION.

on the Loire, a villa in Rome, a Florentine palazzo. The interior would dazzle with ceilings brought from palaces on Venice's Grand Canal, walls enriched by Gobelin tapestries and gilded boiseries. The furnishings—a mix of genuine antiques and reproductions—would be in the style of the Italian renaissance or that of France's Bourbon monarchs. Edith Wharton, in her magisterial New York novel, *The House of Mirth*, recorded the change that the Beaux Arts had wrought on New York's grand habitations: "They were just beneath the wide white facade, with its rich restraint of line," Wharton writes, and then has one of her characters observe: "That's the next stage: the desire to imply that one has been to Europe, and has a standard." In 1897, Mrs. Wharton herself, in collaboration with Ogden Codman, would publish a book, *The Decoration of Houses*, whose intent was to refine that standard. "Proportion is the good breeding of architecture," she would proclaim in that seminal work. No École des Beaux-Arts architect could have said it better.

OPPOSITE AND ABOVE: *Another Vanderbilt mansion is the Burden house at 7 East 91st Street, designed by Warren & Wetmore and completed in 1905. Built for James A. Burden, heir to a fortune based on iron out of Troy, New York, and his wife, Florence Sloane, a great-granddaughter of Commodore Vanderbilt, it was part of the luxurious residential development encouraged by Andrew Carnegie near his mansion at the southeast corner of Fifth Avenue and 91st Street. The Burden house's main elevation, with its three tall arched windows, its graceful consoles supporting a balcony, and its crisp cornice, is a flawless composition recalling the late 18th-century pavilions of Gabriel. The Burden house's 65-foot-long Louis XVI–style ballroom is one of the most exquisite in New York. In it, Whitney Warren deftly employed rose marble, ormolu, and stucco to suggest the ghosts of Versailles.* PRIVATE COLLECTION.

ABOVE, LEFT: *The March 26, 1883 party that inaugurated the mansion that Richard Morris Hunt had designed for William K. Vanderbilt and his wife, Alva, was a turning point in the aesthetic life of New York. Standing at the northwest corner of Fifth Avenue and 52nd Street, the gray limestone mansion, with its echoes of the châteaux of Blois, Chenonceau, and Azay-le-Rideau, immediately made passé the reticent brownstone dwellings with their high stoops in which New Yorkers had lived. Its slender turret, embellished with fleurs-de-lis, may be seen as a proclamation of the coming hegemony of Beaux Arts architecture in New York. This historic house was lost in the 1920s.*
THE PRINTS AND DRAWINGS COLLECTION, THE OCTAGON, WASHINGTON, D. C.

ABOVE, RIGHT: *Alva Vanderbilt Belmont dressed as La Tosca for the extravagant costume ball that Mr. and Mrs. Bradley Martin threw at the Waldorf-Astoria on February 10, 1897.*
COURTESY OF MRS. H. BRADLEY MARTIN.

RIGHT: *The elegant French late Renaissance–style château that Richard Morris Hunt designed for Mrs. William B. Astor—the Mrs. Astor— on Fifth Avenue at 65th Street, was, in fact, two houses. Mrs. Astor occupied one half, while her son, John Jacob Astor IV, lived in the other half. Completed in 1895, the lovely limestone château—seen here in 1902—was leveled in 1926. The site is now occupied by Temple Emanu-El.*
PRIVATE COLLECTION.

OPPOSITE: *Karl Bitter was responsible for the sculpture in Mrs. Astor's gallery-ballroom. When designing the room, Hunt made detailed drawings of every wall to show how the Astor painting collection would look and fit. This ball-room replaced Mrs. Astor's original one at Fifth Avenue and 34th Street which, because it held 400 people, made that number magical for Gilded Age society. The new ballroom held 600.*
PRIVATE COLLECTION.

Stanford White's own house at the northwest corner of Lexington Avenue and 21st Street was an unimpressive brownstone of the 1840s, but its interiors—redecorated between 1895 and 1900— were showrooms of the archi- tect's taste. The drawing room, where he employed the decorator, Allard & Sons, had ruby-red velvet walls hung with paintings attributed to Holbein and other "old mas- ters," French and Italian pilasters and columns, and a gilded Italian ceiling. The doorway led to the dining room. The White house was replaced by the Gramercy Park Hotel in the 1920s.
PRIVATE COLLECTION.

The Italian Renaissance–style Villard Houses, on Madison Avenue between 50th and 51st streets, were designed by McKim, Mead & White in 1882. Their elevations, inspired by Bramante's Palazzo della Cancelleria in Rome, owe a great deal to an assistant in the office, Joseph M. Wells. Commissioned by the German-born railroad promoter Henry Villard, they are, in fact, six separate houses behind a common façade, with Villard's own residence occupying the south wing. This photograph was taken in 1918. NEW-YORK HISTORICAL SOCIETY.

BELOW: *William A. Clark—the "Copper King" of Montana who had bought a United States Senatorship when the office was still appointive—was an astonishing man who built New York's most astonishing Beaux Arts baroque house. Designed by Lord, Hewlett & Hull, with decorative additions by the Parisian architect Henri Deglane, the 130-room palace cost more than $5 million. Soaring past its four stories capped with a high* mansard roof was a tall tower that was of a type usually found on city halls and court houses. After its completion in 1907, the Senator— then in his sixties—moved in with his twenty-something wife and lived there until his death in 1925. Shortly afterward his heirs sold Clark's dream palace and an apartment building went up on the site at the northeast corner of Fifth Avenue and 77th Street.* LIBRARY OF CONGRESS.

ABOVE: *Most of the original interiors of Villard's houses— designed by outside cabinet- makers brought in by McKim, Mead & White—were lugubrious. Following the financial failure of his Northern Pacific in 1883, Villard sold his house to Elisabeth Mills Reid, wife of the owner of the* New York Tribune. *The Reids commis- sioned Stanford White to bring* some glitter into the house, and glitter they got. Among his achievements is the Music Room, where he transformed a plain barrel vault into an elaborately decorated gold leaf ceiling and had John La Farge paint the lunettes at either end of the room. Ever after known as the "Gold Room," it now houses Le Cirque Restaurant.* PRIVATE COLLECTION.

ABOVE, LEFT AND RIGHT: *Among the city's visual delights are the smaller Beaux Arts–style houses found in almost every neighborhood. A charming example is the residence that Warren & Wetmore completed in 1901 at 7 East 86th Street. It was for Francis Key Pendleton, a New Yorker with familial connections to the author of the words of "The Star Spangled Banner." The Pendleton breakfast room was in the subtly elegant French style favored by Edith Wharton and Ogden Codman in* The Decoration of Houses. *The house, with its alluring rooftop oval windows, disappeared after the Second World War.* AVERY ARCHITECTURE AND FINE ARTS LIBRARY.

Most of New York's châteaux were lucky if they had a corner lot, but the one built by the creator of the Bethlehem Steel Corporation, Charles M. Schwab, occupied an entire block bounded by 73rd and 74th streets and Riverside Drive and West End Avenue. Designed by the French architect Maurice Hébert, its Riverside façade closely followed that of the famed 16th-century French château of Chenonceau, which also fronts on a river. Completed in 1907, the mansion held, among other wonders, the largest pipe organ in any New York residence. The Schwab mansion gave way to an apartment building after the Second World War.

LIBRARY OF CONGRESS.

1 2 3

Gilded Age America's infatuation with the Italian Renaissance led architects to scour Italy for architectural elements to use in the rooms they were creating for wealthy clients. A striking example is the drawing room in the house Stanford White remodeled at One Lexington Avenue for Henry W. Poor, the business information publisher. The room's scale is set by its massive ceiling brought from a Venetian palace, while its chief doorway consists of an antique Italian architrave and pilasters. Completed in 1901, the Poor house was demolished and replaced by an apartment building in 1910.

ABOVE: *Following his second marriage in 1896, the traction magnate, William C. Whitney, purchased a house at the northeast corner of Fifth Avenue and 68th Street and engaged Stanford White to redesign the interior. By the time of its grand housewarming on January 4, 1901, more than $4 million had been spent on redecoration and furnishings. The opulent tone of its rooms was set by the stair hall, with its priceless Brussels tapestries, masterfully carved balustrade, and trophy lion pelt beneath its marble Renaissance furniture. After William C. Whitney's death, the mansion became the home of his daughter-in-law, Gertrude Vanderbilt Whitney. Scarcely a month after her death on April 18, 1942, its contents were auctioned off for a fraction of their worth. Five months later, on October 30, the wrecking ball began shattering the palace's marble walls. Within days, the Whitney mansion, like those of the Vanderbilts and Astors, the Poors and the Clarks, was but a beautiful Beaux Arts memory.*

AVERY ARCHITECTURE AND FINE ARTS LIBRARY.

125

Selected Bibliography

Amory, Cleveland. *Who Killed Society?* New York: Harper & Brothers, 1960.

Baldwin, Charles C. *Stanford White*. New York: Dodd, Mead, 1931.

Burnham, Alan, editor. *New York Landmarks*. Middletown, CT: Weslyan University Press, 1961.

Cowles, Virginia. *The Astors*. New York: Alfred A. Knopf, 1979.

Drexler, Arthur, editor. *The Architecture of the École des Beaux-Arts*. New York: Museum of Modern Art, 1977.

Dunlap, David W. *On Broadway: A Journey Uptown Over Time*. New York: Rizzoli, 1990.

Gayle, Margot, and Michele Cohen. *Manhattan's Outdoor Sculpture*. New York: Prentice Hall Press, 1988.

Glueck, Grace, and Paul Gardner. *Brooklyn: People and Places, Past and Present*. New York: Harry N. Abrams, 1991.

Goldstone, Harmon, and Martha Dalrymple. *History Preserved: A Guide to New York City Landmarks and Historic Districts*. New York: Simon & Schuster, 1974.

Henderson, Helen W. *A Loiterer in New York*. New York: George H. Doran Company, 1917.

James, Henry. *The American Scene*. New York: Harper & Brothers, 1907.

Kouwenhoven, John A. *The Columbia Historical Portrait of New York*. New York: Doubleday, 1953.

Lowe, David Garrard. *Stanford White's New York*. New York: Doubleday, 1992.

Lundberg, Ferdinand. *America's 60 Families*. New York: The Citadel Press, 1937.

McKim, Mead & White. *A Monograph of the Work of McKim, Mead & White, 1879–1915*. New York: Architectural Book Publishing Co., 1915.

Mayer, Grace. *Once Upon A City*. New York: The Macmillan Company, 1958.

Moore, Charles. *The Life and Times of Charles Follen McKim*. Boston and New York: Houghton Mifflin Company, 1929.

Roth, Leland M. *McKim, Mead & White, Architects*. New York: Harper & Row, 1983.

Schuyler, Montgomery [edited by William H. Jordy and Ralph Coe]. *American Architecture and Other Writings*. Cambridge, MA: Belknap Press, 1961.

Shopsin, William G., and Mosette Broderick. *The Villard Houses: Life Story of a Landmark*. New York: The Viking Press, 1980.

Silver, Nathan. *Lost New York*. Boston: Houghton Mifflin Company, 1967.

Stein, Susan R., editor. *The Architecture of Richard Morris Hunt*. Chicago: University of Chicago Press, 1986.

Stern, Robert A. M., Gregory Gilmartin, and John Massengale. *New York: 1900*. New York: Rizzoli, 1983.

Stokes, Isaac Newton Phelps. *The Iconography of Manhattan Island, 1498–1909*. New York: Robert H. Dodd, 1915. Reprint, New York: Arno Press, 1971.

Tauranac, John. *Elegant New York*. New York: Abbeville Press, 1985.

Vanderbilt, Arthur T. *Fortune's Children: The Fall of the House of Vanderbilt*. New York: William Morrow and Company, 1989.

Wector, Dixon. *The Saga of American Society*. New York: Charles Scribner's Sons, 1937.

Wharton, Edith. *A Backward Glance*. New York and London: D. Appleton-Century Company, 1934.

———, and Ogden Codman. *The Decoration of Houses*. New York: Charles Scribner's Sons, 1897.

Wolfe, Gerard R. *New York: A Guide to the Metropolis*. New York: McGraw-Hill, 1994.

Index